ON
LIVING
WITH
DEATH

D.G. ORCHARD

Grace
&
Down

Front Cover: Oil Painting by D.G. Orchard 2015

Back Cover: A Shadow of My Former Self – Oil painting by D.G. Orchard 2015

All pen and ink sketches by D.G. Orchard 2018-2025
www.deniseorchard.co.uk

Published by Grace and Down Publishing

ISBN: 978-1-917455-50-3

www.malcolmdown.co.uk

To my own Mr Darcy.
Thank you for being the wind beneath my wings.

To my fabulous children,
Joel, Esther and Dan.
I'm so proud of you.

Contents

Foreword

Why have I written this collection of rather sad (to put it mildly) poems, exposing those deep places of heartache and pain following bereavement, without including poems of a more positive and hopeful nature?

For myself, I found the most helpful reading material to be where the author expressed deep grief and devastation without trying to "look on the bright side" I needed to identify with the author at their lowest ebb and to spend time there, rather than being urged to "move on".

A particular phrase resonated from a poem by Cardinal Basil Hume: "Grief cannot be shared, it is mine alone."

Although your grief is your own, you are not alone in having the throat-restricting, overwhelming and excruciating pain which makes you want to crawl into a corner, curl up and die.

I have tried to capture in words some of these feelings, with which I hope the recently bereaved are able to identify. My other wish is that this anthology will help their friends and family to understand just a little of what they are going through, now and in the years to come.

Calm Before the Storm

Results Day.
Hallelujah!
End of treatment.
Five months of hellish infusions.
Recovery on the horizon.
Partial, gradual, lengthy –
we'll be grateful for anything.

The camper van beckons,
travelling with revitalised, mutual respect
and new appreciation for one another.
We'll mark our quarter century together with a
public ceremony.

But why are the hospital staff so subdued today?
What's happened to the usual, perpetual jollity?

Why are they busying themselves as I pass,
heads down in their tasks?
Has someone died?
Surely this is a day of celebration.

Then it dawns.
No, no-one has died.
Not yet anyway.

Platitudes

He's gone to a better place.
Says who?
You,
who still have your partner.
You,
whose children still have a father.
You,
who have someone to go home with
after the funeral.

He's gone to a better place.
Says who?
You,
who feel the need to say something positive.
Is that positive?

Not in my book, thanks.
I'd rather he were back here
to parent our children,
be a wonderful grandparent,
and grow old disgracefully with me.

He's gone to a better place.
Says who?
You,
who says I'm now free to make choices.
Really???
To be a single parent,
make all the decisions,
holiday alone,
support myself and the family,
do all the maintenance.
Great choices.

He's gone to a better place.
Says who?
You,
whom he warned me about.
"Be kind," he said,
"Forgive the thoughtless words.
They mean well."

Fair enough.
After all,
what would I say to someone?

But the next person who tells me
he's gone to a better place . . .

Shattered

Shattered.
Completely shattered.
Not just tired, or exhausted,
but like an old, glass vacuum flask.
Shattered at the core,
no longer functional,
but looking fine from the outside.

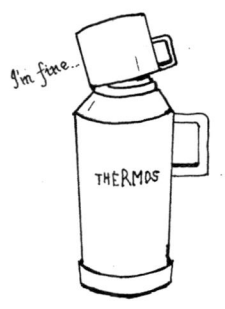

The shell holds it together,
hiding the irreparable,
catastrophic,
internal damage.

My skin holds me together.
I look fine,

I'm still functioning.
My body knows how to move
on autopilot.
But the spark has gone.
No inner flame to light up my smile,
or shine through my now dull, glazed eyes.
Just raw pain
and jagged edges.
Splintered, fragmented,
no use to anyone.
Completely and utterly
shattered.

... just
shattered
inside
into tiny
little pieces

One Flesh

"And the two shall become one flesh."
(Mark 10:8)

Joined.
Bonded
like Siamese twins
through love,
commitment,
children,
the trials and joys of life together.

My other half, so we say.
Joined at the seam.
Bad enough.

A gaping wound on one side,
bleeding and leaking until time
stitches the ripped seam back together.

It's worse.
Becoming one flesh means much more.
Your very fabric is interwoven
like plant roots intertwined.
Impossible to uproot one without the roots of the
other
being ripped
and stripped bare
of life-giving soil.

Deprived of sustenance and protection,
comfort and love,
and precious companionship.

Insides torn apart,
nerve endings exposed,
organs struggling to function.
Ribcage taut,
feeling of being strangled.
Breathing a conscious effort.

Life blood leaking,
leaking everywhere.
Where is it all going?
It must be bleeding into my heart
because my heart is so, so heavy.

Father of the Fatherless

"Father of the fatherless and protector of widows."
(Psalm 68:5)

"The LORD is near to the broken-hearted
And saves the crushed in spirit."
(Psalm 34:18)

"My God, my God, why have you forsaken me?"
(Matthew 27:46)

"Father of the fatherless?"

My father died
mere months after my husband.
I felt nothing.
Impossible to notice a drop of rain
in an ocean of grief.

"Protector of widows?"

Anxiety overwhelms me.
How the children are coping?
Can I manage financially?
The printer's not working.
The Wi-Fi keeps dropping out.
Dripping tap, leak in bathroom,
car battery flat.
The list goes on.
On and on and on.
I feel deluged,
desperately treading water,
in danger of drowning,
yet almost too numb to care.

"Near the broken-hearted?"

"My God, my God,
Why have you forsaken me?"
I feel abandoned, broken-hearted,
but feel no comfort.
I can't find you.
No sense of your presence anywhere.
Certainly not near, like you promised.

"And saves the crushed in spirit?"

My flesh is too alive,
Broken, tender and bleeding,
leaking far too many tears and pain.
But my spirit feels dead.
Crushed, shrivelled and nowhere to be found.

Where are you, God, when I need you?
How can I sing your praises
when I don't trust you anymore?
My guitar is just gathering dust,
my voice gone with the wind.

I'm fighting a lone battle of survival,
an orphan,
abandoned,
feeling punished.
I'm crushed,
husbandless,
fatherless
and waiting
for comfort, protection
and for you to grace me with your presence.

Fix You

I'm a fixer,
a good fixer I like to think.
Here's a problem.
OK . . . let's think about this.
How about . . .
Sorted!

Here's a problem.
But it's beyond my remit.
Can the GP fix it?
No.
How about the consultant?
No.
Chemo?
No.

I will try..

to fix you

Here's a problem.

My problem.

Bereavement.

Can I fix it?

No.

No solution.

Period.

Seems I'm no longer a fixer.

Where Do I belong?

Now that you've gone
where do I belong?

In my house?

This sizeable, spacious,
family home.
Once a hive of activity,
buzzing with family, children, friends.
Sometimes too many!
Now eerily calm and quiet,
with sole occupation.

In my town??

My friends are all couples.
Difficult to smile as I listen to their
plans for the weekend,
or holidays,
together.
I'm the odd one out.
Single,
one half of a couple remaining.
Remembered sometimes,
pitied always.

In my garden??

There's no-one left to grow for,
to admire my beautiful rows of vegetables.
Or to delight in the taste of fresh, home-grown
produce.
No-one to turn everything into wine . . .
even the onions!

In my art group??

You were my best critic,
and my biggest fan.
The joy of painting has vaporised,
along with my odour-free paint-thinner.

With my in-laws??

But I'm not a blood relative.
My children are,
but do I still belong?

So where do I belong in this life?
I'm alone, directionless,
left with the paraphernalia of married life.
Fatherless children to support.
All of us in a fog of shock, heartbreak and sorrow.

But
I am needed by the children,
So I choose to live,
to limp on.
Bruised, still bleeding,
lonely, rudderless.
But alive.
Just.

Daylight Robbery

40 years of full-time work.
providing for family.
Late marriage,
soon blessed with three additions.
No time to wait at that age.

Just emerging from teenage trials.
So looking forward to retirement.
Quality time together at last.
Just the two of us,
exploring in the camper van.
Nothing to argue over
apart from the SatNav.
Endless supersets of Backgammon,
cycle rides, walks,

romantic meals,
cosied up in the van with fake candles.

My last birthday with you,
camping in a cow field.
A stroll to the beach at dusk.
Short cut back through a sewage farm,
(you take me to all the best places).
Curry in the van,
your favourite.
Away from the world,
content and happy,
revelling in each other's company.
Hoping for another 25 years together.

You didn't make it to my next birthday.
A significant one,
meant to be a special celebration.
It certainly was significant.
Cards piled up,
unopened, mocking.
No celebration,
just shock, grief and devastation.

We've been robbed.

How Can I Breathe Without You?

One day after the funeral.
How am I?
In shock.
Alone and isolated.
A rubber band around my windpipe,
suddenly aware of the effort of breathing.
Breathe, breathe, breathe.
In, out, in, out . . .

One year after.
How am I?
Still in shock.
Feeling alone and isolated.
Rubber band slightly looser.
Keep breathing . . .

Two years on.
How am I?
Sometimes in shock.
Often alone and isolated.
Surprised to find I'm still breathing,
almost without effort.

Three years on.
How am I?
Less in shock,
slightly stronger.
Feeling less alone and isolated.
Still breathing.

Does it get any better?
Yes.
And no.
Depends when you ask.
But I'm still breathing.

Welcome Home

Approaching the station.
Anticipation as the announcement is made.
"The train is now arriving in Totnes."
Scanning the platform,
a huge smile and kiss.
Relieved of my
heavy case,
a candlelit dinner
waiting.
My trip was great,
thanks,
but it's lovely to
be home.

Welcome home!

" Totnes,
This is Totnes"

Approaching the station.
"The train is now arriving in Totnes."
No anticipation, no expectations,
just dread and sadness.
No need to scan the platform,
no-one waiting.
A forced, fake smile,
weaving through the greeting couples,
pretending everything's fine.
A huge effort to hold back the brimming tears.
My case as heavy as my heart.
An empty house,
cold and dark.
No smell of cooking,
no candles.
Just a pile of junk mail.

Welcome Home!

Witness

I'll witness it for you.
Your firstborn,
finding his vocation at last.
Industrial Rope Access.
Getting paid for
abseiling off
very tall buildings.
Not "a profession" in
our day!
So many years
of struggle,
trying to inspire him.
Wanting to put a rocket in a
certain location.
But how proud you would
be now.

"Hey Dad,
I'm getting
paid to do
this!"

I'll witness it for you.
Your daughter's life-time ambition achieved.
A professional dancer on cruise ships,
touring the world.
So many challenging teenage years.
So many hours,
so much money spent.
But how proud you would be now.

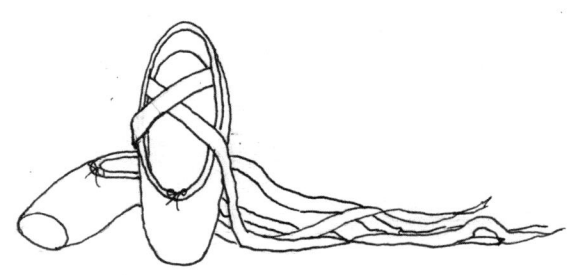

I'll witness it for you.
Your youngest son in further education,
a red-brick university no less.

His mind opened,
challenged by his
subject.
Past the usual teenage
challenges.
Now he "gets it",
gets what you were
about.

Sad not to be able to discuss so many ideas with you.
How proud you would be now.

I'll witness it for you.
Your wife,
turning her hand to writing.
Sadly, material provided by you,
by your untimely death.

Why Didn't I?

Why didn't I
tell you how much I respected you?
Your wisdom,
your logic,
your calmness.
A perfect foil to my frequent overreactions and
emotions.

Why didn't I
tell you how proud I felt to be seen with you?
How good it made me feel,
to walk into a room with you
and be so pleased to introduce you
as MY husband.

You were very much
"the wind beneath my wings".

Why didn't I
tell you how handsome you were instead of
pointing out your defects?
Your growing belly,
greying hair,
thinning eyebrows,
eyes looking a bit strange.
(Were these signs that I failed to notice?)

Why didn't I
tell you what a good father you were?
Despite teenage clashes
and our countless disagreements on strategy.
The children are creative,
dynamic, adventurous,
questioning, challenging,
and most of all, kind.
Great qualities,
inherited from you.

Why didn't I
tell you what an amazing husband you were?
Even with your sometimes impossible demands,
always asking just a bit more than I felt able to give.
Hard-working, responsible,
intelligent, interesting,
dynamic and loving.

Why didn't I
tell you how much I admired you?
Your acceptance of everyone,
Your effusive welcome to visitors.
Anyone, any time.
Never too tired to give of yourself,
even whilst your life was ebbing away.

Why didn't I
tell you just how much I loved you?
You were the only one for me.
No-one else came close.

Why didn't I tell you?
Why oh why didn't I tell you?
Why on earth did I not tell you?

Perhaps I did.
I just can't remember.
I'm tormented by guilt,
weighed down by regrets,
steeped in doubt about myself.
Did I measure up?
Was I a terrible wife?
Was I kind enough?
Demonstrative enough?
Appreciative enough?

I'm left with the insecurity
and heartache,
of not knowing
if I told you
just how special you were.

Life Goes On

A maternity ward on a busy road.
Roar of rush-hour traffic.
Emergency vehicles
racing in all directions.
All oblivious to my momentous, overwhelmingly
painful,
struggle
to bring new life into the world.
For some reason the world didn't pause,
Or even notice.
Life just goes on.

Now my lover, my best friend,
my very heart
has left me.

Another momentous occasion.
But this time death, not life.
Farewells, condolences,
then for others,
life just goes on.

Five years on.
Painting, teaching, gardening,
tennis, choir.
Usual enjoyable, distracting activities.
Three fabulous grown-up children,
all with different aspects of our combined
personalities.
Such a joy to see their father emerging
in different guises.
So much to be thankful for.

Yes,
life goes on.
But with a hidden, underlying, permanent
sense of loss,
pain still piercing to the core.

So deep,

yet tears always lurking at the surface.

A full pool

waiting for the slightest opportunity to spill over.

Yes, life does go on.

Sort of.

Moving On

"She Never Moved On"
I've heard said of widows.
Mmmmm . . . So . . .
Exactly what does that mean?
Simply shed 25 years of the strongest bond on earth?
Married to my own Mr Darcy,
everything I dreamed of in a life partner.
Both completely committed to our life together,
deepest places entrusted to one another,
to cherish or abuse,
'til death us do part.

Three children
all with a piece of him,
reminding me daily of his vibrancy,

his humour, his looks, his intelligence.
His eccentricity,
his faults.
His life.

He appears in my dreams.
He's left me for someone else . . .
No, he's here, we're making up.
He holds me, we kiss.
"I'm so glad you're back!"
An overwhelming sense of relief and joy.
All is well.
Then I wake up.

So what should I do to "move on"?
Stop sleeping
to prevent the nightmares?
Abandon my children
to remove all the evidence?
Ignore the constant pain,
like toothache in the chest?

Life continues,
filled with activity to distract.

The periods of distraction grow longer,
the raw pain eases.
But the pain of loss of my life and love remains.

So "spoiler alert",
I'm going to disappoint you!
I'll probably never "move on",
Whatever that means.

Four-Letter Words

Endless YouTube videos,
some great,
many painful.

"How to clear the swimming pool."

Chlorine, shock doses,
PH raiser, PH reducer,
alkaline raiser, alkaline reducer,
flocculent,
stabiliser,
algicide,
water hardener,
skimmers,
leaf baskets,

pumps, filters,

pool return valves.

****, ****, ****!

Where do I start?

Where are you when I need you?

"How to change a rear car brake light."

Easy, 5-minute job.

Find the model.

Undo special screws –

Oops, one's dropped down into a deep crevice,

totally unreachable.

****!

Identify which is correct bulb to replace –

5 minutes.

Retrieving special screw –

2 hours.

Check brake light works.

Foot on brake

but can't see rear light.

Need another person.

Where are you when I need you?

"How to refill a printer cartridge."

Use syringe with special green adapter.
Where and what on earth is the green adaptor?
Alternative method – syringe air into bottle of ink.
Remove syringe.
Fountain of magenta over me, the wood floor,
everywhere except on the newspaper.
****, ****, ****!
New white blouse
looks like the Chainsaw Massacre.
Printer still not working.
****!

Endless maintenance and problems.
Thank goodness for YouTube.
But where are you when I need you?
I've never sworn so much.

Irritations

It's so irritating that . . .

The loo seat is left up.
The wet shower curtain is bunched up,
yet again,
left to go mouldy so I have to keep washing it.
As if I don't have enough to do.
A mound of clothes draped over your chair,
rendering it invisible
and spilling onto the floor.

You invade my domain
by working on the kitchen table,
just because your office is so messy.
You crash into the bedroom

shouting a cheery
"Good Morning"
an hour before I have
to get up.
You know it's not my
best time of day!

My Mr Messy

You excitedly open a
new parcel,
spreading packaging
and parts everywhere.
Then can't find the
instructions.

Life is much more orderly now.
The loo seat remains down,
the shower curtain stays clean.
The chair is clearly visible,
the office neat and tidy.
My kitchen is my sole domain.
My mornings are so peaceful and undisturbed.
New packages and parts are neatly laid out,
complete with instructions.

But how I so long to be irritated again.

What Now?

What now?
After far too many family deaths
and premature widowhood.
Children are off travelling
hoping to escape the pain,
completing the fracturing of a once close-knit family,
where I truly belonged.

Who now?
A widow.
An ex-wife.
A distant mother.
No longer needed almost every second of the day
to tidy, to sort,
to listen, to comfort, to give advice.

To act as a punchbag for their frustrations, anxieties
and uncertainties.

Now a newly-christened single person,
launching herself into a long-forgotten
and completely scary world.
Rudderless, fragile, unsure.
Longing to travel,
but not alone thanks.
Vague hopes of a new companion,
but not a shackle.
Someone who will gently blow the wind beneath
my wings.
Someone like my husband.

We

We.
Such a small word.
Apart from "I" and "a", none smaller.
A tiny, little two-letter word,
packing such a powerful punch.

We
leaps out of social media,
overshadowing whatever amazing activities are
being posted.
Bandied around with little thought
by those who still belong
to that someone special.
To the rest of us
it bites,

it stings,

it accuses.

Another arrow piercing a lonely soul,

or a forever-broken heart.

We.

Enjoy it whilst you can.

One sudden day you may be plunged

into the ranks of the inferiors.

The Singles.

The Saddos.

Those who try not to be bitter,

but who long to be able to use that tiny, little word.

Postscript

So where am I now,
9 years on?

Still breathing.
Still dreaming my husband is alive after all,
though for some reason he always seems cross with me.
I tell him I'm angry too
because he left me.
How could he do that to me?

Children are blossoming and maturing before my eyes.
We are close,
perhaps closer than we would have been.
As the years go by we are able to laugh more and
remember together.
We are thankful for all he has given us,
warts and all.

I feel a great weight of responsibility towards them,
often unable to help enough with advice and support.
I'm limited and would like to pass them over to their dad,
aware of how much more use he might have been.

But I need to be kinder to myself.
I can only handle so much
without that oh-so-precious support and love
of a life-partner.
I'm doing my best.

My faith in God, though sorely tested, has returned.
It's different,
it's quieter,
less black and white.
Hopefully less judgemental.
After all, what do we *really* understand?
Thoughtless platitudes and verse quoting are out.
The reality is God *can* heal,
but mostly doesn't in this life,
at least not in the way we would like.
But I'm accepting of that.
Just about.

I appreciate each day.
My love of gardening has resurfaced,
having died along with Ed.

I paint, I cook, I sing, I bake bread.
I play tennis.
You name it, I do it!

But I still get taken by surprise by tears
surfacing at some unexpected trigger.
They should be buried deeper now,
but they're not.

I know many who have found happiness with new
partners.
For me, that's unlikely.
There will never be another Ed,
but I try to live out his favourite saying:

"If you can't be with the one you love,
love the one you're with."

In other words,
appreciate those friends and family you do still have.
I'm trying!

Denise Orchard 2025

Acknowledgements

Thank you to friends who have read my poems and encouraged me to go ahead and publish them.

Thanks to Swanwick Writers' Conference who deemed an entry from one of this collection worthy of a prize. This was another encouragement.

Thanks to Liz Carter at Capstone Publishing Services who helped me over the final hurdle of formatting and actually getting the job done, after far too many years of facing a brick wall.

About the Author

Denise is a retired teacher, living in Devon. She gave up her flat and a career in a merchant bank in the City of London and moved to Exeter 40 years ago after becoming a Christian. She had found a wonderful group of other believers and wanted to join their caring and inspirational community, as well as to enjoy the beautiful scenery and coastline of the South West.

It was here she met her husband-to-be. She was inspired to start writing this collection of poems two years after his sudden death, after 25 years of marriage. They were on the point of retiring and looking forward to having quality time together, with the third and youngest child about to go off to university.

She has since resumed a full and active life, travelling, playing tennis and piano, singing, walking, writing, reading, gardening, cooking and painting. Her husband appears in her thoughts most days, sometimes with sadness, though with much less anguish than in the early days of bereavement, but mostly with happy memories which make her thankful for those years of marriage. He is still her inspiration in many ways.